IMAGES
of America

ALONG THE
CAPE FEAR

This book is dedicated to
Tabitha Hutaff McEachern,
a good friend of
Cape Fear Museum Associates

A young boy watches the wonders of the Cape Fear River, *c.* 1880.

IMAGES
of America

ALONG THE
CAPE FEAR

For the Billos –
With my very best
wishes,
Susan Taylor Block

Susan Taylor Block

ARCADIA

First published 1998
Copyright © Cape Fear Museum Associates, 1998

ISBN 0-7524-0965-4

Published by Arcadia Publishing,
an imprint of the Chalford Publishing Corporation,
One Washington Center, Dover, New Hampshire 03820.
Printed in Great Britain

Library of Congress Cataloging-in-Publication Data applied for

Rufus Morgan photographed this scene on the Cape Fear River in 1873.

Contents

Acknowledgments

Many people have contributed to the creation of this book. I am particularly thankful for the assistance of Janet Seapker, Harry Warren, Timothy Bottoms, Suzanne Ruffin Roth, Melva Calder, Grace Russ, Dana Twersky, Case Newberry, Amy Hooker, Ed Turberg, Ann Hewlett Hutteman, Jonathan Noffke, Diane Cashman, Dr. James Rush Beeler, Merle Chamberlain, Beverly Tetterton, Joe Sheppard, Caronell Chestnut, Dr. Anne Russell, Tabitha Hutaff McEachern, Mary Alice Jervay Thatch, Valerie McIver, Brenda Marshburn, Hugh Morton, Isabel James Lehto, Tom Grainger, Leslie Bright, James Bartley, Joseph W. Taylor, Betty Hill Taylor, Virginia Jennewein, Floyd Howell, Addie Dunlap, Sadie S. Block, David E. Block, Tom Lamont, Robert Chestnut, Hannah S. Block, Kenneth M. Sprunt, the late Mary Scott Bethune, Hannah K. Wright, Martin S. Willard, Gibbs Willard, Neal Thomas, Howard Loughlin, Garvin D. Faulkner, Jean Hall Wessell, Henry B. Rehder, Stanley Rehder, Terry Horton, the late John Hall, Skinny Pennington, Anna Pennington, Peggy M. Perdew, Delmas Haskett, H. Thompson King III, Lorraine Fleishman, Ethel Botesky, Millie Botesky, Beverly Jurgensen, Leslie N. Boney Jr., Hugh MacRae II, Walker Taylor III, Joe Reaves, the late Atha Josey Jones, Bobbie Marcroft, Sallie Josey Crawford, Sue Boney Ives, Russell James, Judy Fussell, Dr. Walter Campbell, Marilyn Pierce, Tony Rivenbark, Jack Ashby, Isaac Grainger, Katherine Rhett Fox, Laurence Sprunt, Jack Travis, Hilda Worth, Catherine Solomon, Vernell Moore Smith, Annie Martin Artis, Rabbi Robert Waxman, Andy Wood, Samuel D. Bissette, Joe Bennett, Lucretia Thornton McDaniel, Frances Thornton Reynolds, Albert Corbett, Betsy Burney Wright, Thomascenia McKoy, and Col. Edward P. Bailey.

On a more personal note, I wish to salute the memory of my grandmother, whose stories made the past exciting and with whom I spent many happy hours poring over old photographs. I am also grateful to my husband, Frederick L. Block, for his patient assistance and humorous asides; and my daughters, Taylor and Catherine, just for being.

Susan Block

Introduction

In the solid brick basement of Cape Fear Museum, where neither moths nor rust are allowed much corruptive power, 10,000 images of the Lower Cape Fear, in the form of photographs, postcards, and drawings are catalogued, preserved, and stored. It seems fitting that such treasures are housed deep in a Work Projects Administration structure built originally as a National Guard Armory. (In fact, a few yards away from the photographs, there sits an eerie, quiet 80-foot-long underground firing range.) It seems fitting because the images belong now to the people of New Hanover County, but most are rare photographs that deserve to be in a garrisoned vault. So that the community may enjoy a sampling of what usually is viewed by trained professionals, a series of three books is planned in celebration of the museum's centennial. *Along the Cape Fear* is an overview of the collection. The other two volumes will feature historic structures that no longer exist and images of area beaches.

To be a history buff and to be set loose in the collection was a great pleasure, but to join image to information was even more fun. Wilmington has been blessed with many good historians and such a wealth of public resources as the downtown "Research Triangle": the Lower Cape Fear Historical Society, the New Hanover County Library, and Cape Fear Museum. In the case of one individual, a picture source was also a reference source—the late Louis T. Moore, who was a tireless photographer and chronicler. Local history mavens Janet K. Seapker, Ann Hutteman, Diane C. Cashman, Dr. James Rush Beeler, Merle Chamberlain, Beverly Tetterton, Ed Turberg, Delmas Haskett, Bill Reaves, Gibbs H. Willard, Harry Warren, Jonathan Noffke, and Dr. Chris Fonvielle were all very helpful.

Personal interviews were the icing on the research cake. They took place everywhere from Hall's Drug Store to the Victorian parlor of the Latimer House. Usually the interviewees spoke in soft Southern accents complete with rounded vowels and dropped *R*s, pronunciations that are disappearing rapidly from Wilmington's linguistic landscape. Photographs can be very provocative, however, and often the responses were stronger than the accents. Sometimes the sight of an old picture would call up sentimental memories long forgotten and occasionally evoke unprintable tales so eccentric and funny that we can only hope they will be passed down verbally as long as the sun rises in the east.

Sadly though, this project often reminded me of the human resources lost to us in the 23 years I have been doing local historical research. I remembered interviews I conducted in the 1970s with Mary Hannis Whitted, John Hall, Ruth Worth, Thomas "Mickey" Hall, Jessie Newbold, Fannie deRosset, and Henry MacMillan. I thought wistfully of the courses I took under Claude Howell and Dr. B. Frank Hall (speaking of accents) and all the new questions I would like to ask them. More than once, I wished I could consult with Dr. E. Lawrence Lee, Ida Brooks Kellam, Billie McEachern, Ruth Walker, Elizabeth McKoy, Dr. Robert M. Fales, and Crockette Hewlett. But it all combined to make me appreciate even more the sources available.

Occasionally memories, photographs, *and* artifacts connected in wonderful extraneous stories that would not fit the word allowance for the image. For instance, when the old post office was demolished, photographer Eric Norden bought the tower clock. Smaller in size than I expected, but big in decibels, it had tolled the hour for 45 years to all of downtown Wilmington.

It was news to me when the expert on Wilmingtoniana, Virginia Jennewein, first told me the clock story a few months ago. I visited her at her antique shop, just across the street from the new, chimeless post office.

"Have a seat," she said in her inimitable voice. "I think that chair is sitdownable." I showed her a photograph by Eric Norden and, among other things, she told me the story of the clock.

"He put that clock in the guest room of his house. Needless to say, visitors never stayed more than one night."

Later that day, author Bill Reaves concurred. "Eric Norden lived on Wrightsville Sound. When that thing bonged, you could hear it all over the place."

I could hardly wait to phone the museum registrar, Tim Bottoms, and relate my newfound little story. "We've got it," he said calmly when I finished talking.

"You've got what?" I asked.

"The clock. It's just around the corner. You walk by it every time you go to the photograph collection."

I couldn't resist a quick trip by the museum. Sure enough, there stood the ancient timepiece, exposed gears and all. I assume that after Mr. Norden's death, his widow, Laura Howell Norden Schorr, gave the clock to the museum. She was, after all, a highly trained musician and had probably heard enough bonging.

The tales, objects, and images all are noteworthy, but the true stars of this book are the photographers. Though many are responsible for the work in the collection, a few deserve special mention: Henry Cronenberg, Rufus Morgan, Alexander Orr, Charles Yates, Clinton and Cornelius Van Orsdell, Hugh Morton, George Nevens, Louis T. Moore, Henry Sternberger, Barbara Marcroft, Henry Bacon McKoy, William A. Williams, John Kelly, Thomas Artis, James B. Swails, Herbert Howard, W.M. Shaw, Jack Dermid, and Mr. Norden. Together with others less prolific and some who will always, unfortunately, be anonymous, they have used cameras to record instantly what historians labor long to describe. Their acute powers of observation are often evident in what they chose to capture. Sometimes they froze the historic moment. Sometimes they sensed something mundane might be important. And sometimes they simply saw the poetry that is Wilmington.

One
A Little Chronology

The dateline of the photographic collection at Cape Fear Museum begins in 1847, when an unknown photographer crouched beneath a black tarp and laboriously captured on a glass plate a Market Street scene. Between that faded shot and a crystal clear image of Wilmington native Michael Jordan lies an abundance of visual material that often invites an avalanche of explanation. Editorial constraints make it impossible to enumerate the puzzling questions that surround the 1847 photograph, the wartime experiences of Captain John Newland Maffitt, the genealogical connections between many subjects, and the superfluous stories that enliven the images and a host of interesting facts. But in many ways the pictures speak for themselves.

Dating from 1847, this is the earliest known photograph of Wilmington and the earliest outdoor image of North Carolina. At the time, St. James Church was new and still had all its finials, the wood fence at Dr. Thomas Henry Wright's house was in apple-pie order, and the latest horse-drawn contraption was proudly displayed. (Courtesy Amon Carter Museum; Fort Worth, Texas.)

Steeples, some now unfamiliar, punctuate the 1880 Wilmington skyline as a boat nears Point Peter on the west side of the Cape Fear River. Once the "College Road" of local navigation, the stretch of river from Point Peter to Eagles Island was known in old deeds and state documents as the "Thoroughfare."

Ties and millinery were required dress for this picnic at Hilton, just north of downtown Wilmington, dating to about 1898. The donor's identifications include "Mrs. Galloway, Mrs. McClure, Mr. McClure, M.S. Bunting, Miss Galloway, Miss Jenkins, Mr. Munson, Miss Cooper, Mr. Bunting, Mrs. Elmison," and several unidentified children.

On February 6, 1879, Professor Dare twice walked a tightrope 60 feet above Market Street. He walked both forward and backward and, at intervals, on his hands. He fell once, but caught himself with one arm. A local reporter wrote that it was "perilous enough to satisfy the most morbid appetite . . . A vast multitude witnessed the performance, but perhaps the greater number declined to remain and see the most difficult of his maneuvers—the taking up of a collection for the benefit of the poor."

Wilmington photographers C.W. Yates and A. Orr captured this lonely soul walking the trestle of the railroad bridge in 1880.

Belgian block leads to a group gathered on South Front Street at the intersection of Market, *c.* 1880. Towers of the City Market can be seen on the right.

The jewel of North Front Street in 1880 was the Bank of New Hanover (later People's Bank) on the northwest corner of Princess Street.

The market, seen in the distance at the foot of Market Street, still stood in 1880 but was demolished the following year.

Imar ibn Said, better known in Bladen County as Prince Moreau, was a household slave of Gov. John Owen. He learned English, converted to Christianity, and translated parts of the Bible into Arabic for his family back home in Sudan. He was offered freedom and passage home, but Prince Moreau chose to remain with Governor Owen. He died in 1858 and was buried in the Owen family cemetery.

Alexander Manly, editor of the *Daily Record*, and his brother Frank (shown here leaving work) enjoyed quiet rides through the city. Probably the same carriage took the Manlys on a trip of terror when they fled Wilmington during the Riot of 1898.

Alexander and Carrie Sadgwar Manly had their son christened in 1903. Mrs. Manly was the daughter of Frederick Sadgwar, a Wilmington master carpenter and cabinetmaker. She won acclaim in her own right when she toured in the 1890s as lead soprano with the Fisk (University) Jubilee Singers.

The Murchison family collection (four images are reproduced here) at Cape Fear Museum is rich in depictions of leisure activities. This precursor to the "Piney Woods Festival" took place about 1896.

"All dressed up and nowhere (much) to go." A group sits on the pier of the Carolina Yacht Club, probably watching a turn-of-the-century regatta and looking forward to some Southern-style refreshments.

Golfing form has changed through the years; the links at Cape Fear Country Club have also. In 1896, the course was located at Hilton, and part of it doubled as a baseball field in the summer.

They must have been pretty good in their day, for they had a gallery, but just think what some aerodynamic clothing might have done for their game. Alas, in 1896, "Nike" was merely the Greek goddess of victory.

Natalie Jackson and Preston Royster were married December 23, 1962, in St. Stephen's A.M.E. Church. Pictured are, from left to right, Owen Jackson, Dorothy Bailey Johnson (mother of Natalie and Owen), Natalie Jackson Royster, Preston Royster, and Susie Royster (mother of the groom). The mother of the bride later became the first African American elected to the New Hanover County Board of Education. After her death in 1984, she was memorialized in the naming of Dorothy B. Johnson Elementary School.

Pearl Dixon married William Leonard Balthis on December 28, 1907. Mrs. Cyrus Hogue Jr. of Wilmington is a niece of the bride.

It was "eight maids a-posing" on the occasion of Herbert Borden and Mary Maffitt's wedding at St. James Church, April 8, 1896. The groom became vice president of the Atlantic Coast Line. The bride was the daughter of celebrated Confederate Navy hero Captain John Newland Maffitt. These people are, from left to right, as follows: (bottom row) Callie Maffitt, Lola Martin, Carrie Maffitt, Mary Meares, and Maggie McPherson; (top row) Mary Burr, Mary Bridges, and Maud McLeod.

Robert Strange married Mary Reid Taylor on April 21, 1920, at St. James Church. He was the son of Bishop Robert Strange and the great-grandson of Dr. Thomas Henry Wright. The bride was the daughter of Allan Taylor and the granddaughter of John Allan Taylor and Catherine Harriss Taylor. The bride's gown, orange blossom headband, and satin pumps are now part of the museum's permanent collection.

Jane Meares Williams wore Scottish garb to dance the Highland Fling in a production of *Kirmess* at the Opera House (Thalian Hall). It was one of a series of amateur plays staged by Mrs. George Kidder and the Colonial Dames in 1896 to raise funds to erect the memorial obelisk at Fourth and Market Streets to Cornelius Harnett, Revolutionary patriot.

Jane Williams MacMillan's children, Henry Jay MacMillan (third from right) and Helen MacMillan, joined William Whitehead to create murals at Thalian Hall in 1939. Mr. MacMillan, a graduate of the Parsons School of Design, was commissioned to paint a mural in Rockefeller Center. During World War II, he documented the activities of the European front in paintings that are now in the permanent collection of Cape Fear Museum.

Showing a marked resemblance, the daughters of Thomas Davis Meares, a local attorney and rice planter, pose for William A. Williams in 1900. They are, from left to right, as follows: Jane Iredell Meares Williams, Catherine Grady Meares Harriss, Margaret Iredell Meares Latimer, Frances Iredell Meares Green, and Eliza Walker Meares.

Mrs. W.T. Daggett, Roxanna McNeill Worth, and Julia Stickney Worth (from left to right) create a study in faces and hands in this engaging 1902 portrait. Mrs. Worth's husband, David Gaston Worth, was a wholesale grocer and the only local coal merchant after the Civil War. The Worth house still stands at 412 South Third Street.

B. Frank Hall and Thomas Hoke Hall, sons of John Hall, made their own space in 1915 behind the house where Frank seems to be "holding forth." It was a trait he turned into a distinguished career as professor of philosophy and religion at the University of North Carolina at Wilmington (UNC-W) and as a Presbyterian minister esteemed for the intellectual content of his sermons and admired for the sonorous quality of his voice.

Sadie Stadiem was two years old in 1908 when she dressed as Little Red Riding Hood for a community play in Kinston. She moved to Wilmington in 1926 as the bride of Nathan Ellis Block, a Baltimore native who had recently opened a shirt factory with his father and two brothers.

"Snakes and snails and puppy dog tails . . ." William Worth (far left) and Charles Worth (third from left) posed in 1902 at Shandy Hall, the summer home of their grandfather, David Gaston Worth. Both boys became Presbyterian missionaries—William in Africa, and Charles in China.

In 1957, as in many other years, Sue McKoy, Elizabeth McKoy, and Adair McKoy (from left to right) enjoyed the geejoggle at 402 South Third. The onomatopoeic contraption was once a common piece of porch furniture in Wilmington. It could be converted into a seesaw or a sliding board, but its most popular function was as a squeaky, bouncing seat.

Frank Herbst took young Julian Morton (1896–1945) on a spin up Princess Street about 1907. Mr. Herbst owned an automobile dealership. Julian Morton eventually became president of Hugh MacRae and Company and the Linville Company.

To escape the stifling summer heat, Judge Joshua Grainger Wright moved to "the sound" like these young Wilmingtonians a century later, pictured here, about 1900. Wrightsville Sound was named for Joshua Wright's extensive land holdings that included what is now Airlie and many of its neighboring subdivisions. When the closest beach attracted enough attention to be named, "Wrightsville Beach" seemed geographically appropriate.

Shell Road.

In 1886, the Sound Turnpike was paved with sun-bleached shells and became known as the Shell Road until county officials named it Wrightsville Avenue. Another road covered in shells is pictured here as it appeared *c.* 1900: Market Street. On the left is the entrance to the National Cemetery.

Even the horses look quizzical about this float in the 1910 Elksfest parade. Though 30 years before the movie debut, Frank Baum's book, *The Wizard of Oz,* was all the rage and had become a musical comedy. Perhaps the horseman on the left is Wilmington's answer to the Tin Man.

The Elks, a thriving organization in 1910 when this particular beast was "bagged," had been so since 1902 when a distinctive building was erected at 255 North Front Street. A metal elk head once graced the facade, but it moved with the Elks to the Governor Dudley Mansion in 1945.

Members of the Dreher, Rehder, and Schulken families cruised South Third Street in a car bedecked in roses. Behind them is City Hall, completed in 1858, but more famous for its theater than for its role in municipal government. Thalian Hall was fitted originally with 188 gas burners for illumination and an iron tank in the ceiling, holding "very many barrels of water," as a sprinkler system. Today, upfitted in every way, Thalian Hall flourishes under the veteran directorship of Tony Rivenbark.

In 1910, Delgado Mills was proud of its Amherst Ginghams and Triumph Cottons but will be remembered longer as the setting for Robert Ruark's fictional bestseller, *Poor No More*. Ruark, whose father worked at the mill, wrote, "It is customary to say that the characters in this book bear no resemblance to anyone, living or dead. That would certainly be a lie, but working out just who is who is bound to be difficult."

Children gathered on Wrightsville Beach in 1916 for the Feast of the Lanterns, a short-lived annual event held at Lumina, the dance pavilion that once was the pride of Wrightsville Beach.

One Feast of the Lanterns beauty queen was Miriam Holladay, pictured here about 1916. "She was the prettiest girl in town and she and Arthur Bluethenthal were very much in a situation of star-crossed love," said neighbor Marilyn Pierce 80 years later. "I saw him walk up on her porch at 414 Nun Street in his blue French Flying Corps uniform to tell her goodbye before he went off to war."

Arthur Bluethenthal, pictured here about 1918, was born in Wilmington in 1891 and educated at Princeton, where he twice was an All-American football player. He later volunteered for the French Aviation Foreign Legion before the United States entered World War I. When his plane was shot down on June 5, 1918, at Coivrel, France, he became New Hanover County's first war casualty. In 1928, the local airport landing strip was named for him and is still called Bluethenthal Field, if only by natives.

After Mr. Bluethenthal's death, Miriam Holladay married Goodlett Thornton, beloved president of Wilmington Savings and Trust. "My father believed in a hometown bank," said daughter Frances Thornton Reynolds. "People came to him who really did not qualify for credit. If he believed in them, he would make the loan. It almost always worked out."

Eric Norden snapped many pictures of life on Wrightsville Sound in the 1920s. Although most subjects suffer from anonymity, the photographs are valuable for other reasons. Some record a quaint element of daily life. Many capture local fashions and mores. A few are amusingly contrived, like the one above, which Mr. Norden entitled, "Falling for Photographer."

Like people from every walk of life, violinist Laura Howell Norden Schorr (1902–1985), seen below, enjoyed the delightful awfulness of crabs—the thrill of netting the unevolved monsters, the challenge of getting them into the bucket without losing human flesh to their steel blue claws, the strange horror of dumping them into a boiling cauldron as they snap and wriggle, and the hedonistic high of savoring warm Carolina lump crabmeat doused in melted butter.

This is a duck hunt at "The Camp" at Orton Plantation, about 1925. The people are, from left to right, as follows: (bottom row) Lincoln Hill (chauffeur), Theodore G. Empie, and J. Laurence Sprunt; (top row) "Captain" Asa Burris (manager of Orton), Charles E. Taylor, Louis Hall, Charlie Delts (hunting guide), Frederick W. Dick, Joe Voight (hunting guide), unidentified, and Samuel Simpson Nash.

This Brunswick County hunter encountered more than a mallard in 1901. Alligators grow to a length of 10 to 12 feet in the Cape Fear, and somewhat smaller ones have been found in Greenfield Lake.

Photographer Eric Norden (on right) posed with two other men at the grave of Eleazer Allen in 1900. Mr. Allen was buried on the grounds of "Lilliput," his riverside plantation just north of Orton and was one of the "Family," 15 politically powerful, interrelated grantees who collectively owned 80,000 acres of land in southeastern North Carolina in the early 1700s. The dining room table at Lilliput sported 12 solid-gold finger bowls.

With the help of his four-footed "crew," Fred Willetts Jr. rode in his wagon-drawn skiff in the 1928 Feast of the Pirates parade. Alice Hart, the Willetts's maid, oversaw the voyage. The little buccaneer grew up to captain the family business, Cooperative Bank for Savings, serving many years as president and later as chairman of the board.

Children aside, if the Feast of the Pirates had had an official verse, it might have been the one commonly sung in area taverns long ago. "If claret be a blessing, / This night devote to pleasure; / Let world's cares and state affairs / Be thought on more at leisure; / Fill it up to the top, / Let the night with joy be crown'd, / Drink about, Love and friendship still go round." After only three years, the Feast of the Pirates was held no more, in part because city fathers thought too many participants had been excessively "crown'd" with joy.

A 1940 Buick leads the way across a rustic Bradley Creek bridge. The banner overhead heralds the upcoming Miss North Carolina pageant at Lumina: "North Carolina's most beautiful girls will cross this bridge July 17th."

Assuming an array of postures and dress, bathing beauties competed at Wrightsville Beach in the 1920s. Lumina was the venue for varied competitions, including boxing and wrestling matches and greased pole climbs.

The joy of romping! In 1910, it was even more pleasurable than today, considering that water and breeze constituted air conditioning and, at the time, sunshine was considered more a prescription than a health hazard. Today the Blockade Runner Hotel has replaced the Ocean Terrace, seen in the background, and at least a half dozen bathing suits could be made from the fabric of just one of these.

Jimmy Dorsey, Cab Callaway, Harry James, Louis Armstrong, and Kay Kyser were just a few of the musicians who played at Lumina. Gene Krupa, the greatest of the Swing Band drummers, performed in the ballroom in the 1940s and was photographed by Hugh Morton, grandson of Lumina builder Hugh MacRae.

The strand just east of the Boardwalk at Carolina Beach looks crowded in this photo taken about 1960, but chamber of commerce officials were not entirely happy with the picture Hugh Morton took, insisting that the beach usually was more crowded.

Could a picture be worth a thousand questions? Probably not, but a few certainly come to mind

when viewing these local 1920s mishaps caught by George Nevens.

Photographer Thomas Artis took this picture of his beloved alma mater, Williston High School, not long before the original building burned in 1936. Williston was an all-black senior high from 1928 until 1968, when area schools were fully integrated and it ceased to be a high school.

Formal wear merchants must have been happy about this 1960 debutante ball at Williston High School. The annual event was organized by Bertha Todd and sponsored by Alpha Kappa Alpha sorority.

Wilmington historian Louis Toomer Moore (1885–1961) posed with an antique bicycle in this 1950 picture, but he usually was on the other side of the camera. He chronicled his beloved hometown with 800 photographs from the 1920s through the 1940s, most of which now belong to the New Hanover County Library. In addition to numerous articles, he authored a popular book, *Stories Old and New of the Lower Cape Fear*. As early as 1896, bicycles similar to this one were marketed locally by Thomas H. Wright. Horses were still the main mode of transportation and Mr. Wright was obviously appealing to a clientele that might have ridden one nag too many. "Buy a Waveler," he advertised, "and you will never be ashamed of your mount." (New Hanover County Public Library.)

Here are the Wilmington Pirates, 1929.

The following poem was first published in the *Christian Science Monitor* and reprinted in the *Wilmington Morning Star* on February 8, 1943.

Greenfield Lake
by Ulrich Troubetzkoy

Here in the hush of seasons,
broomstraw leans
red-gold as the beard of Bohemund,
and the pale plumes of dog-fennel nod,
graceful as courtiers,
in the wind.

The flat boughs of the dogwood,
as if remembering legends, now
bear bloodstained leaves
and scrub oaks burn
under the shining long-leafed pines,
polished with noon.

Soundless, the copper needles fall from cypresses
to their own image in the water,
black swollen roots and slender branches,
swaying with Spanish moss.

The clustered yaupon berries glow,
but the unripe fruit of crisp-leaved holly
forecasts a winter without snow,
and high on the skeleton trees are hung
the druid pearls of mistletoe.

Claude Howell snapped this picture of Serge and Ulrich Troubetzkoy in 1942 at Wrightsville Beach. Serge, a Russian prince, trained at Camp Davis to serve in France. Ulrich published seven volumes of poetry, four of which have won national awards.

Someone turned the camera on artist Claude Howell on the same outing. Mr. Howell's notebooks, now part of the Cape Fear Museum collection, contain photos that form a pictorial diary of his life and a record of local sites.

Long before becoming U.S. president, actor Ronald Reagan won the popular vote at the 1959 Azalea Festival. His official post at the time was public relations representative for General Electric. Harbor Island resident and G.E. distributor Walker Martin was responsible for Mr. Reagan's invitation to the port city.

Azalea Festival Queen Polly Bergen (in sunglasses), Hannah Block (seated, center), and Henry Rehder (standing, arms folded) enjoyed the Rehder's garden in April 1956. Miss Bergen herself, the spokesperson for Pepsi, gave festival sponsors no cause for concern. However, a few early queens kept local rotary phone dials spinning with rumors of royal skinny dipping and other titillating indiscretions.

Virginia Hamilton MacQueen served up narcissus on Cottage Lane for browsers at the 1955 Azalea Festival art show. She and artist Hester Donnelly were instrumental in forming St. John's Art Gallery in 1962. Other charter leaders were Glasgow Hicks Jr., Chatham Clark, Ann Bell, Alex W. Fonvielle Jr., Etta F. Williams, Beulah Meier, Dan Cameron, Robert Calder, James McKoy, Henry B. McKoy, and Mrs. J.A. Bridger.

Wilmingtonians Michael Jordan and Hugh Morton crowned Lynda Goodfriend Queen Azalea XXXV, ten days after freshman Jordan sunk the winning shot in the 1982 ACC Tournament. Michael Jordan, either playing basketball or simply walking across a room, is the human intersection of power, intelligence, and grace. Hugh Morton, North Carolina photographer-at-large, has been capturing history for more than 50 years. In his spare time, he works to preserve and promote the beauty of North Carolina and manages his own "piece of the rock," Grandfather Mountain.

Emily Sue Walton posed at Airlie Gardens during the 1956 Azalea Festival. Pembroke Jones's widow, Sadie Green Walters, created Airlie Gardens with the assistance of Rudolph A. Topel (1860–1937), a horticulturist who had once been a gardener for the German kaiser. They supervised the planting of a 250,000 azaleas and 5,000 camellias in the spirit of Ruskin, who saw the perfect garden as a retention of beauty that springs from the divine carelessness of nature. E.T.H. Shaffer wrote in his 1937 book, *Carolina Gardens*, "At Airlie, there is never a straight line, never the slightest hint of artificiality, no obvious seeking after effect, but Nature, wooed with an understanding heart, has responded graciously, revealing here her happiest moods."

Henry B. Rehder put the finishing touches on the 1959 queen's float and presented Debra Paget with a fresh bouquet. For six decades, Mr. Rehder has been a fixture of cultural life in Wilmington. As a leading florist, the keeper of an elegant garden, and an avid collector of North Carolina art, he personifies the popular needlepoint slogan "Bloom where you are planted."

Stanley Rehder, Henry's brother, appeared on the *Today* show in 1976 to introduce Barbara Walters and 90 million viewers to the Venus's flytrap. The botanical oddity was first noted in 1759 by North Carolina Governor Arthur Dobbs, who recognized its rarity, called it a "Catch Fly Sensitive," and sent one to Europe. John Ellis, an eminent naturalist, saw it and wrote, "I shall call it Dionaea Muscipula, which may be construed into English, with humble submission both to critics and foreign commentators, either *Venus's Flytrap* or *Venus's Mousetrap.*"

Only tradition documents George Washington's resting under this tree on April 24, 1791, but longstanding oral history always bears noting. A Philadelphia newspaper of the day did report that the 59-year-old commander-in-chief traveled down the Post Road, now Highway 17, on that date. Surely he rested somewhere.

The tree pictured here about 1944 at Pleasant Oaks plantation in Brunswick County probably took root before Giovanni Verrazano was born. The French explorer visited the Lower Cape Fear in 1524 and noted it was "full of mightie great woods . . . replenished with divers sorts of trees, as pleasant and delectable to behold, as is possible to imagine." Pleasant Oaks, once the rice plantation of John Allan Taylor, builder of the marble house at 409 Market Street, now is owned by the Bellamy family.

Two
Images of Work

In 1728, William Byrd, the founder of Richmond, Virginia, wrote, "Surely there is no place in the world where the inhabitants live with less labor than in North Carolina. . . . To speak the truth, 'tis a thorough aversion to labor that makes people file off to North Carolina where plenty and a warm sun confirm them in their disposition to laziness for their whole lives."

Perhaps Mr. Byrd had fallen victim to a certain intercolonial jealousy, or maybe he did not travel far enough south in the land of the longleaf pine. Labor and commerce have always been integral to life along the Lower Cape Fear.

The Smithsonian, pictured here in 1929, was located on the southwest corner of Sixth and Campbell Streets. It was the first black-owned gasoline station in Wilmington. Hubert and Mabel Smith also ran a grocery store and cafe.

After the Civil War, Alexander Sprunt and Son Champion Compress transformed Wilmington into an international cotton exporting port. It employed 800 people and had offices in England and Germany. In the 1880s, when this photograph was made at the company wharf, up to 4,000 bales a day left Wilmington on schooners, steamers, railroads, and carts.

The Champion Compress machines had the capacity to squeeze 3,000 bales of cotton to half its original size to save freight charges.

Steamers, like this one that docked in Wilmington about 1918, were loaded night and day at the warehouse wharf. (Special Collections, Duke University.)

The elite cotton tiers of Champion Compress posed in 1900 with their characteristic white gloves. Compress owner James Sprunt defended them with his own life during the Riot of 1898, and gave credit for his attitude to his mother, Jane Dalziel Sprunt. For many years, Mrs. Sprunt spent Sunday afternoons teaching black children reading, writing, Bible lessons, and the Presbyterian catechism.

In the eighteenth century, Greenfield Lake was "Greenfields," the home of Dr. Samuel Green. The old mill still stood in the late 1800s, and was located where the spillway now flows. Mayor J.E.L. Wade and Mrs. Rufus Hicks recognized the potential of the old plantation and led a campaign for its beautification in the 1930s.

The scene looks rural, but in 1890, the R.C. Orrell Livery Sale and Exchange Stables were located on the southwest corner of Third and Princess. The northern parcel of the property was razed in the 1920s to make way for the Wallace Building. The southern section once was the address of William Hooper, signer of the Declaration of Independence. Hooper's ballast stone wall still exists.

W.H. McEachern, a wholesale vegetable and fruit distributor, has been supplying produce to Wilmington for 100 years. Pictured are, from left to right, W.H. McEachern Jr., Sug Powell, and Lina McEachern McCarley in the Water Street office they occupied in the 1920s.

Wilmington's picturesque Historic District once abounded with sights like this one, captured *c.* 1900 on the west side of the 100 block of South Front Street. Dr. Charles Nesbitt (on right), public health officer, fought wealthy landlords and City Hall to clean up tenements and vacant property. His efforts dramatically reduced local cases of malaria and typhoid. (Special Collections, Duke University.)

David William Bulluck and fellow medical students try to make light of a grisly lesson at the University of Maryland, where Dr. Bulluck received his degree in 1873. He was one of only 18 physicians practicing in Wilmington in 1895. In 1900, he introduced the first X-ray machine to the Lower Cape Fear.

In 1912, Dr. Bulluck (1853–1914) and his son, Dr. Ernest S. Bulluck, had a medical office that looked too pretty to be antiseptic. Ten years after his father's death, Dr. Ernest Bulluck became the chief surgeon and owner of Bulluck Hospital at 209 North Front Street, a 24-bed institution that was the forerunner of Columbia Cape Fear Hospital.

James Walker Memorial Hospital Nursing School's graduating class of 1919 were, from left to right, Edna Ann Walton, Clara H. Lowry, Eva I. Canady, Mary L. Stanley, Bessie High, Christine Radcliff, Sadie McCallum, Sula A. Boney, Cora M. Ide, and Clyde H. Benton. The turn-of-the-century hospital was replaced by New Hanover Memorial Hospital in 1967.

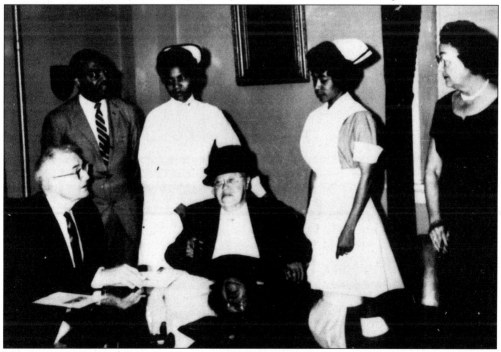

Mayor O.O. Allsbrook bestowed honors on Salome Taylor, director of nursing for Community Hospital, about 1961. Community Hospital, located first on North Seventh Street and later on South Eleventh Street, served the black community from 1920 until 1967.

If cameras had been around, this photograph could have been taken in 1740 as well as in 1890—little had changed. The monotony and physical rigor of field work were skewered by heat, humidity, and mosquitoes. After emancipation, even those reaping the highest rewards soon learned that harvesting crops earned paltry wages. (N.C. Division of Archives and History; N.C. State Museum of Natural History Collection.)

In 1918, the Lower Cape Fear was the largest strawberry- and lettuce-producing area in the world and came in second in peanut production. Here, peanuts are stacked for drying at Orton.

Around 1909, Hugh MacRae and several European agents started five colonies near Wilmington and peopled them with accomplished agrarians from Holland, Italy, Germany, and Poland. Some businesses thrived, like Ludeke and Tinga. Here, escapees from Hitler's regime pose about 1939 at their new home: reclaimed Van Eeden farm in Pender County. (N.C. Collection, University of North Carolina.)

Not too long ago, you did not have to be a farmer to have livestock in your yard. Backyard chicken coops provided many a Wilmingtonian with fresh eggs and Sunday dinner roasters. In this 1912 scene, Jane MacMillan sits with feathered friends at the corner of Wrightsville and MacMillan Avenues in Winter Park.

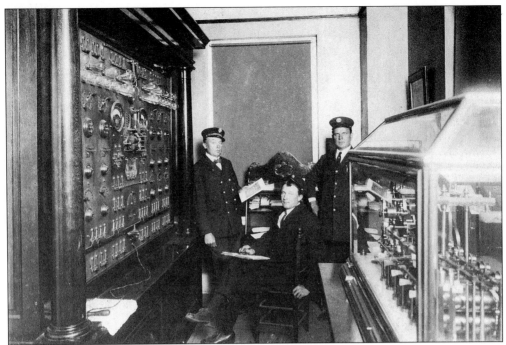

Appearing to have no patience with false alarms, Chief Charles Schnibben, George T. Williamson, and Assistant Chief William P. Monroe man the station at 20 South Fourth Street, about 1899. The building pictured had accommodated horse-drawn engines and was demolished just after the turn of the century to construct a new station with wider doors and updated alarm systems on the same site. The bell on display at Fourth and Dock is all that is left from the old building.

Chief Schnibben "always rode behind a beautiful black horse hitched to a black buggy trimmed with red that ran smartly down the street, whether to and from a fire or on a simple jaunt during the dinner hour," said Henry Bacon McKoy. Chief Schnibben and Assistant Chief Monroe both died in accidents that occurred en route to a fire.

An iron balcony afforded a great view of progress, 1910-style. "But the fire engine was the thing to see and watch for. On each was a tall upright brass or nickel boiler . . . the pumps gleamed with brass and nickel and were always kept immaculately clean and brightly polished," wrote contractor and author Henry Bacon McKoy, who never forgot that he once wanted to be a fireman.

Firemen scramble to the sixth floor of the Atlantic Trust and Banking Company building at Front and Market Streets in 1918, possibly as participants in a statewide firemen's tournament. "The town turned out in masse," wrote Henry Bacon McKoy of such events. "Men stopped all work, nurses grabbed up the little babies and lined the streets to see them go by or to follow after them."

As headquarters for the Atlantic Coast Line, Wilmington was once centered in a web of rails and a network of imposing office buildings.

This was the view looking south on North Front Street in the late 1930s.

This was a typical Atlantic Coast Line office in 1906. "Inside those buildings, things were not all that glamourous," said a former stenographer. "They were dark and drab. Many of the men chewed tobacco and sometimes in the catwalk they didn't bother with a spittoon. The exhaust from all the steam engines added to the smell. . . .There were more pleasant places to work in Wilmington, but no one could match the salaries the coast line paid."

Ella Mae Bullard, Beth Vann, Betty Hill (standing from left to right), and Marie Conley (seated) worked in the Freight Traffic Department of the Atlantic Coast Line in 1948. Their office building on Red Cross Street was spared the wrecking ball and now is occupied by the Wilmington Police Department.

The engine was already an antique when Captain John Harper purchased it to pull the "Shoo Fly," a railway at Carolina Beach that operated in the early 1900s. Iron cowcatchers looked like metal mustaches and were attached to the engine to keep stray creatures and debris from derailing the train.

This 1883 engine weighed 70,000 tons and spewed ebony smoke like a rhythmic volcano. Ladies complained of the soot, but diesel engines never matched the percussive charm of steam engines. Many of these beautiful machines were broken up for scrap metal during World War II.

Wade Chestnut (on right), the father of Wade Jr., Robert, and Bertram, began work at the Atlantic Coast Line loading logs for wood-burning engines. By the early 1920s, when this photo was taken, he was fueling locomotives with coal. Soon he became a railroad engineer and was able to give his three sons a jump start in the automotive repair business.

Bertram Chestnut Jr. (left) and a workman pose with their car "ambulance" at Sixth and Campbell in the auto garage that Bert, Wade, and Robert shared in the 1930s. Wade left the family business in 1949 to work for Wilmington attorney Edgar Yow as developer of Ocean City Resort on North Topsail Island.

In 1925, drug raids conducted by the New Hanover County Sheriff's Department were usually woodsy affairs. Here, Sheriff George C. Jackson (holding pistol) and his deputies ruin a moonshiner's day.

In 1920, the Frank Thompson family posed in front of what truly looks like a "cottage industry." Naval stores like the ones Mr. Thompson processed on Eagles Island were once numerous and strategic to the economy of Wilmington. The rich resin of the longleaf pine was processed and sold to be used in paint, medicine, caulking, and many maritime products.

Today we look across the Cape Fear River and see the USS *North Carolina*, but this is how Eagles Island looked in 1920. Named for Richard Eagles, who purchased the land in 1739, the island has been a rice plantation, a site of Revolutionary gunfire, a thoroughfare for George Washington, a hand-to-hand combat battlefield during the Civil War, and, since 1961, has been the home of a battleship memorial that has attracted more than 9,000,000 visitors.

J.E.L. Wade delivered an address aboard the floating Fergus Ark restaurant at the foot of Princess Street about 1959. Jimmy "Hi Buddy" Wade was a former mayor, state senator, and beloved character-at-large. The Fergus Ark gained notoriety and its own painted purple heart after the *North Carolina* dealt it a glancing blow in berthing.

Harbor Island was marshland before 1925 when Shore Acres Development Company built retaining walls and added 350,000 cubic yards of soil. By 1929, when this picture was taken, the island had a handful of residents and a 2,000-seat auditorium.

Hugh MacRae, the major stockholder in the local power company and trolley car system, came up with a truly bright idea when he conceived of this seaside attraction, pictured under construction in 1905. Workers adorned its hipped roof with lights, and Mr. MacRae named it aptly—Lumina. The ballroom measured a whopping 6,000 square feet and the verandas added another 15,000. The strand itself served as an annex when movies were shown at night on the beach, within a few yards of the lapping waves.

An 8-inch gusher signaled progress and pleased officials of Wrightsville Beach in 1948 when this photograph was taken. The well could pump 500 gallons of water a minute, more than they ever dreamed would be needed. In August 1997, Wrightsville Beach water consumption averaged 1.5 million gallons a day.

The natural beauty of Wilmington and its surrounding area has often made innkeeping a thriving business and has continually converted a percentage of tourists into residents. The Oceanic, which seemed as much a work of art as a hotel, graced Wrightsville Beach from 1905 until 1934, when it was destroyed by fire.

Most people merely saw vessels on the river in its heyday, like this ship being launched during World War I. Others saw more. J.D. Wood said of philanthropist James Sprunt (1846–1924) and the Cape Fear as follows: "Here was implanted within his consciousness that sympathy for sailors and their hardships, for ship owners and their ambitions, for ship masters and captains

with their far-flung horizons; for merchants and their touch upon the markets of foreign lands, and the poet with his sense of the immensity of the sea, the vastness of the universe, the unity of all as lying in the hand of the eternal God."

In 1920, the Newport Ship Building Company purchased the shipyard south of Wilmington where Greenfield Creek flows into the Cape Fear River. The property had been used by the Liberty Shipbuilding Company during World War I. Most of the Newport ships were 300 feet long and weighed 3,000 tons. The vessel pictured here is the *Col. E.G. Hodgson,* a diminutive 150-foot concrete ship commissioned by the U.S. government.

The *Col. E.G. Hodgson* made its maiden voyage up the Cape Fear on May 5, 1921. The Newport Ship Building Company closed its business here in the summer of 1922, but a division of the same firm would return to Wilmington in 1941.

On December 6, 1941, the eve of Pearl Harbor, the Newport News Shipbuilding Company launched its first Liberty Ship. By the time V-J Day rolled around, 125 more had rolled successfully down the Wilmington shipways.

Many of the ships returned to Wilmington after the war and were harbored on the Brunswick River. In the early 1970s, Horton Iron Company eventually purchased the remainder of the "Mothball Fleet" to market as scrap metal. Terry Horton remembered, "Most of them had simply been sealed shut in the 1940s. Everything inside was just as they left it: flare guns, completely equipped galleys. I remember happening upon a fully equipped operating room. Surgical instruments were still lying there in a tray."

The steamer *Wilmington*, pictured here about 1910, was built in 1880, and actually christened for the city in Delaware that uses our name. The iron vessel was brought south in 1892 to ply the waters of the Cape Fear until 1923, when it was sold and altered into a Florida ferryboat. At the latest report, it was carrying passengers again, this time in Brazil.

The *City of Southport*, pictured here about 1923, was a smaller steamer that handled passenger overflow from the *Wilmington* and continued to run after the larger vessel was sold. It usually stopped at Orton before docking at Miss Kate Stewart's picturesque hotel in Southport.

Captain John Harper, pictured here about 1885, owned and piloted the steamers *Wilmington* and *City of Southport*. He was a beloved character who delighted his passengers by spinning historical yarns, complimenting the ladies, and serving a shot or two of bourbon from the flask he kept hidden in the raincoat that was always draped over his arm.

Southport fishermen grew accustomed to Claude Howell and his sketchpad.

Southport was a quaint village in 1941. Many of its picturesque houses were built by citizens who made their living either navigating the treacherous shoals of the Cape Fear or harvesting the surrounding waters.

Purse boats pooled their resources near Bald Head Island, 1942.

Artist Claude Howell found beauty in fishing nets and soulful honor in the work of the menders. He took this picture in 1942, but continued to photograph and paint them for several decades.

The Wilmington Public Library was inviting but small when it was housed on the second floor of City Hall in 1930. Emma Woodward MacMillan was head librarian for many years. Mrs. MacMillan took a special liking to one young man who spent a lot of time in the library. Others had labeled him lazy. She disagreed and challenged him with books, and David Brinkley has been grateful to her ever since.

Al Dickson, David Brinkley's supervisor at the *Wilmington Morning Star*, snapped this picture of his gifted but exasperating new charge about 1940. Mr. Brinkley's assignments were unchallenging, and it turned their relationship into an amusing game of cat and mouse.

Having issued its first dispatch in 1867, the *Wilmington Morning Star* is the state's oldest newspaper in continuous operation. Housed originally in an office over a grocery store at 3 South Water Street, it moved to 109 Chestnut Street, and then to the Murchison Building, pictured here, where it remained from 1935 to 1970.

The Boys' Brigade was the pet project of Col. Walker Taylor, who founded it in 1896 and nurtured it until his death in 1937. The armory was located on the southeast corner of Second and Church Streets from 1905 until 1950. It was a gift from Mary Lily Kenan Flagler in memory of her father, Col. William Rand Kenan, and contained a gymnasium, a 2,000-volume library, an auditorium, and a bowling alley.

Brothers Warren and Skinny Pennington were flying planes in and out of Wilmington in the 1930s, when aviation was so rustic that nocturnal landings were aided by volunteers who sat in formation inside parked cars with their high beams on to illuminate and outline the runway. Warren, the first licensed pilot in North Carolina, once flew under the old northeast Cape Fear River Bridge unscathed, and his nephew, Jack Bennett, zipped through the hanger at Bluethenthal Field.

Edward Gibbs (center), a former Tuskegee Airman, founded the Atlantic School of Aviation at Bluethenthal Field in the mid-1940s. Brothers Robert and Wade Chestnut Jr., who were already partners in an auto mechanic business, became affiliates in the Atlantic School as well. Their accomplishments were noted in *Ebony* magazine.

Atchison, Kansas, might have had Amelia Earhart, but Wilmington had Anna Feenstra Pennington, the "It" girl of the Cape Fear Museum photograph collection. Married to Skinny Pennington for 55 years, she is now an aviation historian.

When Minnie Evans (1893–1987) began working the ticket booth at Airlie Gardens in 1947, no one dreamed that one day her oil, colored pencil, and crayon drawings would bring prices thousands of times the cost of a tour. During her lifetime, Mrs. Evans's work was exhibited at the Museum of Modern Art in New York, the Portal Gallery in London, and L'Institut de L'Art Brut in Paris. She is pictured here about 1969.

The verticality of cedars and longleaf pines doubles when they are reflected in the liquid mirror of Greenfield Lake. Spanish moss, blooming waterlilies, and azaleas in season heighten an effect which has attracted artists throughout the years. Claude Howell, founder of the Fine Arts Department at UNC-W, used the scene as an exercise for many of his students, including this class in 1942. Behind him is Margaret Tannahill Hall, the first director of St. John's Art Gallery.

Three
Things Military

The soldiers below speak for Wilmington and herald a remarkable collection of photographs depicting military and paramilitary activities in a geographic locale both vulnerable and strong. From the bright red coats of the British occupation during the American Revolution to the camouflage jackets omnipresent when equipment left Wilmington for Saudi Arabia during the Persian Gulf War, the port city has seen more than its share of military and paramilitary affairs.

The World War II greeting here is part of an extensive postcard collection at Cape Fear Museum. (Courtesy MWM Printing, Aurora, Montana.)

Wilmingtonian Captain Joseph Price, of the Confederate Navy, captured the Federal gunboat *Water Witch* on film in 1864, but later that year, Lt. Thomas Pelot gave his life capturing the ship for the Confederacy. The *Water Witch* was burned, stakes and all, by Southern sailors on December 19, 1864, in White Bluff, Georgia, to prevent capture.

This 1909 image of West Point, New York, by Andrew J. Howell would seem out of place here were it not for the fact that the 8-inch, 150-pounder Armstrong gun belongs in New Hanover County. Federal troops confiscated it after the fall of Fort Fisher and sent it north where it still stands guard over the Hudson River.

Thirty years after his death at Fort Fisher in 1865, General W.H.C. Whiting's widow was still wearing black when she posed outside her residence at 111 South Fourth Street. General Whiting was a West Point engineer who moved to Wilmington the day after Fort Sumter fell. He had an unusual personality, but then Katherine Walker Whiting was used to that sort of thing. She was the niece of character-at-large Major Jack Walker, who once seized by the horns a mad bull as it was raging through the streets of Wilmington, threw it to the ground, and held it there.

Major James Reilly was a fiery Irish youth who escaped British oppression by stowing away to America dressed as a girl. He served in the U.S. Army 16 years before switching clothes again, this time to become a Confederate officer. Though a frustrated general, he achieved "local hero" status and earned historians' respect for his fearless combat and intelligent leadership at Fort Fisher. After the war, Major Reilly helped start a Catholic mission church and school in Brunswick County.

Fort Caswell, at the mouth of the Cape Fear, is a massive masonry post built as a federal garrison, 1826–1838. Commandeered by the Confederacy and later captured by the Union, it was deemed by U.S. Rear Admiral D.D. Porter, "almost impervious to shot and shell . . . in many respects stronger than Fort Fisher, and harder to take by assault." Here, World War I soldiers load the big guns.

It is a safe bet that these soldiers, stationed at Fort Caswell in 1904, did not deeply appreciate the aesthetic charms of the place: sea breeze, Old Baldy streaking light through the night, yucca blossoms, windswept oaks, and silver maples showing their metal. However, in 1949, the North Carolina Baptist State Convention did, and purchased it for $86,000. The 248-acre tract continues to be used as a religious retreat.

84

American Legion Post 4 was located on the west side of South Seventh Street between Church and Castle Streets. T.J. Bullock (top row in white shirt) was one of at least 33 blacks from Wilmington who died in World War I.

When just any old car was a rarity, this Packard "18" driven by automobile dealer W.D. MacMillan Jr. in 1911 must really have turned heads. Only 2,493 versions of the full-size "18" were produced by Packard, the luxury car benchmark of the day. Each sold for a whopping $4,200. Mary Wiggins Davis and Alice Davis Peck were two of the maids of honor, all three of whom were granddaughters of George Davis, attorney-general for the Confederacy.

A troop of World War I soldiers stood at different grades of attention in 1918. A gnarled veteran of the Spanish-American War, possibly Thomas Cowan James, joined them. The officer on the far left (foreground, with sword) is Capt. Edward P. Bailey. In the background is Union Station, the Atlantic Coast Line terminal and executive office building that was located on the northeast corner of Front and Red Cross. On an average day, 18 trains arrived and departed from Wilmington.

An Armistice Day celebration was the occasion for this 1919-style traffic congestion.

In 1919, a World War I victory parade passed the Governor Dudley mansion (with portico) and other homes in the 400 block of South Front Street.

Soldiers marching south on North Front Street were eclipsed by the craggy grandeur of the old post office in this 1925 Louis T. Moore photograph. In 1936, suffering a serious preservation lapse, the City had the 1891 stone structure demolished to make way for a bigger facility. It took a force of Wilmington workmen a solid month to tear down what had taken four years to construct. (New Hanover County Public Library.)

In 1920, Cleveland VanBuren Reaves donned a fake beard and brought out his World War I German spiked helmet and revolver for this memorable shot. He was the uncle of Wilmington researcher Bill Reaves, longtime chronicler of Wilmington's history and the author of *Strength through Struggle: A Chronological and Historical Record of the African-American Community in Wilmington, N.C.*

This is the 1932 Wilmington Light Infantry Football Team. They are, from left to right, as follows: (first row) Bubber Hall, Joe Stone, Kenneth Daniels, Lawrence Coley, Tom Bruff, Curtis Matthews, Ed Hawkins, Ernest Beale, E.A. Jones, Herbert Ayers, and Harris Haskett; (back row) Coach Alton Lennon, Norman McKenzie, Gene Clendenin, Vic Stefano, Leslie Williamson, Rivers Hanson, Walker Brown, Fred Tienken, Harold May, Bruce Musselwhite, Jimmy Merritt, Cooney Sellers, Adolph Oterson (WLI treasurer), Dr. R.B. Rodman (trainer), and Jimmy Bordeaux (manager).

World War II brought horrors to the coast of New Hanover County. Guns were mounted in the dunes at Carolina Beach, airplanes crashed offshore, merchant ships were blown out of the water, and bodies washed up on smooth beach sand. Here, like a cat dropping a dead bird on a threshold, soldiers displayed a captured Japanese submarine on Market Street in 1944.

Millie Botesky (left) and Katie Kennedy worked at Camp Davis, at Holly Ridge, during World War II. "We had fun times, too," said Millie. "We had a dance hall and a movie theater. The soldiers had a football team and some of us were cheerleaders. Sometimes when we weren't working, my girlfriends and I would walk to Topsail Beach, swim for a while, and then try to get a ride back to Camp Davis on the 'cattle car,' an 18-wheeler the Army used to transport camp employees."

In 1942, Grace Jarrell Russ enjoyed a floor show at the National Guard Armory, the same building that in 1970 became home to Cape Fear Museum. Mrs. Russ has been a faithful employee of the museum for many years.

As part of Wilmington's USO "HI MOM!" program of the 1960s, Mrs. T.B. Wood phoned Thomas Wood Jr. in Germany, while her other son, Clarence, looks on.

The USS *North Carolina* was brought to Wilmington in 1961 through a campaign led by Hugh Morton, assisted by schoolchildren who contributed thousands of dimes to pay for the move. The bear cub, Hobo, paid a visit in 1972 to promote the idea of a state zoo, and later further distinguished himself as the longtime beau of Grandfather Mountain's "Mildred the Bear."

Exhibiting more than a dash of British reserve, Lord Halifax, British ambassador to the United States, mingled with the crowd in front of City Hall following a review of 350 British Anti-Aircraft troops on December 3, 1943.

Three fighter pilots from Wilmington, Oscar Kenneth Biggs, James Roy Starnes, and George Thomas Rich, posed with Rich's P-51 Mustang aircraft at Fowlmere Field near Cambridge, England, in 1945.

Four
The Faith Connection

The first designated space of worship by settlers in Wilmington was a portion of the *c.* 1740 courthouse. British rule dictated that it be an Anglican service, and a few years later, the crown provided Wilmington with the first St. James Church building. After the American Revolution, religious striation became more obvious; buildings as diverse as local religious persuasions began to punctuate the modest skyline.

Post-Revolutionary buildings gave way to larger structures, and, along the way, many fine churches, both big and imposing and small and jewel-like, were consumed by tongues of earthly fire or felled in the name of progress. Still, a wealth of architectural wonder and inspiring beauty remains. Records of the buildings and the devoted people behind them weave their way throughout the collection of Cape Fear Museum.

In 1761, the Reverend John McDowell reported that the roof of St. Philips Church in Brunswick "is all fallen down again" and added that "the chapel is a most miserable old house, . . . and every shower of rain or blast of wind, blows quite thro' it." The church building was completed in 1768 by donations from parishioners and windows contributed by Governor William Tryon. Hurricanes and the abandonment of Brunswick Town took their toll, and today, just as in this 1890 photograph, it stands true to Reverend McDowell's description.

St. Philips Parish at Brunswick Town was created in 1741 when rivalry with the newer town, Wilmington, was raging. The Reverend James Moir wrote, "A missionary in this river has a most difficult part to act, for by obliging one of the towns he must of course disoblige the other, each of them opposing the other to the utmost of their power." Here, Jeffrey Lawrence, an employee at Orton, stands at the ruins of St. Philips Church in 1895, more than 100 years after Brunswick Town lost the competition.

Mardy MacMillan had been sitting still long enough when the photographer caught her scampering across the grounds of St. James Church after a service in 1909. Margaret Anderson MacMillan, the daughter of W.D. MacMillan and Katherine Gaston deRosset, descended from a long line of senior church wardens.

There were at least three "blackbirds baked in a pie" in this 1932 production by St. James Church kindergarten, directed by teachers Mary Graham and Louisa Howard. They are, from left to right, as follows: (bottom row) Nell Trask, Fred Block, William Ross, Joe Morrison, and Laurence Sprunt; (top row) Fred Poisson, Francis Van Landingham, Blanche Bolles, Rockwell Poisson, and Shirley Finkelstein.

Dr. Thomas Henry Wright built Mount Lebanon Chapel in 1835 to accommodate the growing number of Wilmington families who spent their summers on the sound. Mount Lebanon eventually became the home of Pembroke Jones, who renamed it "Airlie," after his ancestral home in Scotland. The chapel is pictured here c. 1920.

The Temple of Israel, dedicated in 1876, is the state's oldest Jewish house of worship. The local Reform congregation was organized officially under the leadership of Solomon Bear, Abraham Weil, Nathaniel Jacobi, and Jacob I. Macks in 1872, but German Jews had been contributing to the life of the city since 1738. This 1895 image is from the 12-part series *Art Work of Scenes in N.C.*, published by W.H. Parish.

B'Nai Israel was founded in 1898, but their first synagogue was still under construction when members posed in 1913 wearing their Sabbath best. Situated on the north side of Walnut Street between Third and Fourth, the building had an upstairs balcony for women and a mikveh for ritualistic bathing. The Orthodox congregation moved to 2601 Chestnut Street in 1954.

Chestnut Street Presbyterian Church originally was called Second Presbyterian Church, and in 1858 members included Alexander Sprunt and John C. Latta. After the Civil War, attendance waned, and in 1867, a black congregation purchased the Carpenter Gothic building. The roster of the new congregation included distinguished locals William Cutlar, Alfred Hargrave, Henry Taylor, and George Price.

Second Presbyterian Church built a new building in 1873 at 520 North Fourth Street and soon changed the name to St. Andrew's Presbyterian Church. Elaborate preparation went into their 1893 holiday greeting from the members of William C. Von Glahn's Sunday school class. The boys are, from left to right, David Holt, Tommie King, Sam Heide, Lawrence Von Glahn, Walter P. Sprunt, Tommie Lawther, and Alex McClure.

While craftsmen fashioned First Baptist Church, Civil War cannons fired and yellow fever raged. Nevertheless, the Reverend John L. Prichard and layman George R. French encouraged the acceptance of the Samuel Sloan design. This photograph was taken by Rufus Morgan in 1875, possibly from the scaffolding of the Temple of Israel, which was under construction at the time. (N.C. Division of Archives and History; N.C. State Museum of Natural History Collection.)

In 1860, members of the George R. French family assembled outside his home at 103 South Fourth Street. Mr. French, who operated a lucrative shoe business at 116 North Front Street, was a native of Massachusetts. When First Baptist Church needed a bell for its new tower, he sent a fine, old bell to Boston for recasting and presented it to the congregation on December 4, 1871.

First Presbyterian Church had already lost two buildings to fire when this one burned on New Year's Eve, 1925. Though many members of the congregation wanted to replicate the 1861 structure, some of the more well-traveled individuals persevered. By 1928, First Presbyterians were worshipping in the rock-solid Neo-Gothic building that still stands at the corner of Third and Orange; it boasts a sophisticated fire alarm system.

One Gothic aficionado was Dr. A.D.P. Gilmour, minister of First Presbyterian Church from 1922 to 1941. Dr. Gilmour and his wife, Nancy, posed in the manse that was located on the northwest corner of Fourth and Orange Streets. The house was razed in the 1960s.

The children of Benjamin Franklin Hall and Margaret Tannahill Sprunt in 1910 were, from left to right, James Sprunt Hall, Alexander McDonald Hall, Susan E. Hall, Louis Edward Hall, John Hall, Jessie Hall, and Jane Hall. All were members of First Presbyterian Church. The three sisters, Wellesley graduates, spent time in China, where Jessie Hall served for many years as a missionary at a Presbyterian medical station funded by the Sprunt family of Wilmington.

In 1890, the Germania Cornet Band lined up in front of the John Allan Taylor house at 409 Market Street. Members include Engelhard Rehder (drummer on left), John H. Rehder, Will Rehder, and John Gieschen (on leader's left). All were members of St. Paul's Evangelical Lutheran Church, established May 31, 1858.

Services had been going on for four months when St. Mary Catholic Church was consecrated on April 28, 1912, by James Cardinal Gibbons. The Spanish Baroque building was the work of father and son, both named Rafael Guastavino, who orchestrated the fine construction with no steel, wood beams, or nails.

The first baby baptized in St. Mary Church was E. Lawrence Lee Jr. on January 20, 1912. In addition to "rediscovering" Brunswick Town, he authored several volumes of local history, including a peerless standard, *The Lower Cape Fear in Colonial Days*. Pictured in 1949 are Dr. Lawrence Lee, sons Larry and James, and wife, Mary Borden Wallace Lee.

St. Mark's Episcopal Church was designed by William Ralph Emerson and Carl Fehmer, founders of the prestigious Boston Society of Architects, and was built in 1871 by church member Alfred Howe. Mr. Howe also built the Mary Jane Langdon house at 408 Market Street and his own home, distinctive for its mansard roof, at 301 Queen Street.

The picture above was taken in 1935 by photographer and St. Mark's communicant Thomas Hall Artis. As a young man, he worked for Bellamy Drug Company. In the 1930s, he opened a photography studio at Bladen and North Fourth Streets. He was a crucifer at St. Mark's and consistently spent a portion of his income on toys for needy children.

This is St. Mark's communicants class. Three of Wade Chestnut's grandchildren were in the same confirmation class at St. Mark's Episcopal Church in 1955. Mabel (third from left), Robert II (far right), and Wade III (middle row, center) were confirmed in a ceremony led by Bishop Thomas H. Wright (top row, left) and Rector Edwin Kirton (top, right).

St. Mark's Mission School appears here in 1958. Ethel Ellen Bernard (on left) left her secure post as a teacher with the New Hanover County school system to teach underprivileged children from the Brooklyn area of Wilmington. The effort was funded primarily by St. Mark's Episcopal Church, but the entire budget was meager enough to classify Ethel Bernard as a local saint.

The cornerstone of St. Stephen A.M.E. Church was laid in 1880, and the building was constructed by six master carpenters and six master masons, all members of the church. Tony Wrenn, archivist for the American Institute of Architects, deemed the interior of the late Gothic style structure to be "one of the most impressive in Wilmington."

From 1844 until 1886, local Methodists, both black and white, worshiped in the Front Street Methodist Church. After it was destroyed by fire, the congregation moved to Mulberry Street and named their new church "Grace." Mulberry soon became known as Grace Street. Here, some of the young ladies pose for their Sunday school teacher, Eric Norden, in 1910.

Five
Bricks and Mortar

"Poets are born, it is said, not made. Perhaps this is true of those whose imagination is expressed in stone," wrote Anna Nutter, a former teacher at Tileston School, in 1924 on the occasion of the death of her favorite student, Henry Bacon.

Perhaps good architects do carry special imaginative talents in their DNA. It would follow that the dedication of the ardent bricklayer, the plaster worker, the fashioner of iron, the liberating stonemason, and the meticulous woodwright elevates their labor to an art form as well. In addition, developers' dreams and benefactors' gifts emerge in concrete form. The architecture of the Lower Cape Fear is the manifestation of many talents and, though dominated by bracketed Italianate structures, is rich in diversity and laden with tales.

These "bricks and mortar" are seen along the eastern side of South Third Street, *c.* 1945.

At Orton Plantation in 1890, a man had his gun and columns had their guardrails. The original dwelling was built by Roger Moore on an 8,000-acre Brunswick County tract in 1725. The gardens are a popular tourist attraction. (N.C. Division of Archives and History; N.C. State Museum of Natural History Collection.)

When Orton Plantation was featured on the cover of *Southern Accents* magazine, assistant producer Frank Capra Jr. took notice. He and movie mogul Dino deLaurentiis were looking for a location for their upcoming film, *Firestarter*, and the Brunswick County plantation eventually won out over mansions in Italy, Mexico, and Texas. Some scenes actually were filmed at Orton, but this facade is what went up in smoke when Drew Barrymore stared it down. *Firestarter*, filmed in 1983, was the first major motion picture made in Wilmington, but picturesque settings, vintage buildings, low-cost labor, and lenient regulations have turned the port city into Hollywood East.

This photo provides a magnificent view of the Burgwin-Wright House. John Burgwin, a well-connected lawyer and merchant, purchased the lot on the southwest corner of Third and Market that had been the site of the local jail or "gaol." Mr. Burgwin set a fine Georgian house on the foundations in 1771 and contracted to sell it to Captain Thomas Wright, the owner of Fairfield Plantation in present-day Wrightsboro. The buyer died in 1771 and the seller moved to England during the Revolution. In 1799, the buyer's son, Judge Joshua Grainger Wright, purchased the house, where his descendants lived until 1869.

A Colonial-era underground passage built to contain rambunctious streams runs from the Burgwin-Wright House to the Cape Fear River. It was probably similar to Jacob's Run tunnel, which measures 24 inches by 6 1/2 feet and runs diagonally from Fifth and Princess to the foot of Dock Street. This photograph was made by Herman Benton, a *Wilmington Morning Star* photographer, in 1972.

The house at Winnabow Plantation, pictured here as it appeared about 1897, was built on a 27,000-acre tract by Daniel Lindsey Russell in 1840. His son, Daniel L. Russell Jr., was born there in 1845. Though the father owned 200 slaves, the son culminated a legal and political career by running for governor on a strong civil rights platform. With good support from the poor, he was elected on the Republican ticket and served North Carolina from 1897 to 1901.

Spanish moss waved over Mr. and Mrs. Cornelius Thomas and their son, Neal, at Clarendon Plantation in 1943. Clarendon, located on the Brunswick side of the Cape Fear River, shares its name with a nearby 1664 Barbadian settlement that lasted only three years.

Claude Howell took this 1947 picture of the 1817 Bald Head Lighthouse on his way to sketch driftwood on the shore of what was once known as Smith Island. The oldest beacon in the state first used an oil-fueled light to cast a 16-mile beam.

In this photograph from the 1930s, Kenan Fountain dominates the intersection of Fifth and Market before being scaled down by architect Leslie N. Boney to accommodate increased traffic. The fountain was shipped in 30 railroad cars to Wilmington and erected on the site. Behind it stands the Carolina Apartments, built in 1907 and the lifelong home to Wilmington's most famous artist, Claude Howell.

A little snow is a big thing in Wilmington. Nothing was moving but the shutter when Bobbie Marcroft photographed Market Street from the Bellamy Mansion in the 1940s. The contrast shows off the tracery patterns of Hart and Bailey, a nineteenth-century Wilmington ironworks.

Fancy as an antebellum grand dame, the Bellamy Mansion, built in 1859, graces the northeast corner of Kenan Plaza, with balconies within its piazzas and columns fit for a Corinthian palace.

Claude Howell and Norman Hall posed by First Baptist Church in 1922. Though the church was most famous for its 197-foot spire, the angle of this photograph accentuates the building's strength. With 46-inch buttresses and 38-inch walls, it is not an illusion.

As if tatted by Vulcan, lacy ironwork adorns the gate, stairs, and porch of the Eilers House at 124 South Fifth Street. The Italianate house was built in 1852 by Herman B. Eilers, a commission merchant who was a partner with neighbor Jacob Wessel in a grocery and liquor business.

Oakdale Cemetery was organized in 1852 in a health-conscious attempt to move local burials far from civilization. The entrance, near the corner of Thirteenth and Rankin, was accessible only by a dirt road. Oakdale Lodge, seen on the left, *c.* 1900, was the work of architect James F. Post. Deemed a financial burden, it was partially dismantled in 1915. Stone from the foundation now lines a nearby plot.

The Wood family built it, but Hugh MacRae embellished the house in 1905 (pictured here as it looked about 1900) with the help of friend and architect Henry Bacon. Naming 713 Market Street "The Castle" seemed natural. Mr. MacRae's grandfather, Alexander MacRae, owned a fortified house on the southeast corner of Front and Princess Streets known as Dunnegan Castle.

The three-story house that once stood on the northwest corner of Third and Market was built by Armand John deRosset. "I remember the day President Taft came to town," said Marilyn Pierce. "It was 1909 and I was five years old. At the time, there was a porch on the first floor and my mother lifted me out onto the roof of it so that I could see the president."

Marilyn DeVany Pierce also posed for this picture when she was five years old. She is the great-granddaughter of Captain Benjamin Washington Beery, a shipbuilder who constructed a number of vessels for the Confederacy. His house still stands at 202 Nun Street. From the belvedere, one can see the site of his shipyard two blocks west.

Students and faculty members posed in 1880 in front of Tileston School. The 1871 building was the brainchild of legendary teacher Amy Morris Bradley, a native of Maine. It was designed by New England architect John A. Fox, and financed by Bostonian Mary Hemenway, a Unitarian philanthropist. A plaque to honor Amy Bradley still hangs in the main hall. It begins, "Though of northern birth . . ."

In 1884, the "Upper Room" on the second floor of Tileston Normal School held student assemblies, as well as Thalian Association productions.

A dirt road still led to the Front Street Atlantic Coast Line bridge in 1900.

The Bonitz Hotel was located at 120 Market Street. In 1890, a room's rent was $1.50 a day.

Silversmith Thomas W. Brown was in residence at 114 Orange Street when this nineteenth-century photograph was taken. The 1805 structure housed a World War II–era restaurant before it became home to St. John's Museum of Art.

This is the Finca Room at St. John's, seen on February 22, 1963. The people in this image include, from left to right, Emma Woodward MacMillan, Louise Washburn, William Whitehead, Emma Bellamy Williamson Hendren, and Dick Meares.

The ancient gates at Airlie once served as portals for gardens in France and Newport. Sadie Jones Walters and son-in-law John Russell Pope brought them to Wilmington about 1920. Mrs. Walters's Airlie home eventually grew to contain 38 apartments for guests, a ballroom, and a banquet hall. Sir Walter Raleigh's newel post and rail adorned the main staircase, and a letter penned by George Washington hung on the wall.

In the early 1950s, the Colonial Apartments (left) and the YMCA occupied the northeast corner of Third and Market Streets. Here, the apartment building has just suffered a fatal fire.

Like taking a house tour in a time machine, the camera allows us to view interiors dismantled long ago. The dining room (pictured here about 1940) at 416 South Front Street, home of the M.W. Divine family, would today be a collector's dream and a housekeeper's nightmare.

The Murchison House, at 305 South Third Street, was built in 1876 by David R. Murchison, a Confederate veteran who was heavily involved in a handful of Wilmington's most successful businesses. This photograph probably was taken about 1890.

The Solomons share a meal in February 1897 in their home at 701 Market Street. They are, from left to right, as follows: Sigmond Solomon, Helen Solomon, unidentified, Ida Solomon, and Harry Solomon. Sigmond Solomon came to Wilmington from Bavaria in 1861 and, with his brother Bert, operated S & B, a wholesale and retail dry goods business on the southeast corner of Front and Market.

A single bald bulb illuminated this dressy Wilmington dinner party, about 1900, probably held at the Howell House, 702 Market Street. Andrew Howell Jr. was a Presbyterian minister, the author of *The Book of Wilmington*, and the father-in-law of photographer Eric Norden.

Henry Bacon designed and built "The Rocks," a dam that closed New Inlet. Made of 16,756 gross tons of granite and constructed from 1875 to 1889, it deepened the channel from 7 to 16 feet. In the right foreground are William Beery McKoy and his future bride, Katherine Bacon, daughter of Henry Bacon.

Henry Bacon Jr. collaborated with F.H. Packer to design the 1924 bronze Confederate Memorial in the plaza at the corner of Third and Dock. The granite was quarried in Salisbury, North Carolina, and purchased through salesman John Ernest Ramsay. Mr. Packer was so impressed with the stone salesman's strong facial features that he used him as the model for the soldier. Henry Bacon Jr. was better known for designing another monument involving a subject with strong features—Abraham Lincoln.

The phrase "keeping up with the Joneses" specifically meant emulating the lifestyle of Sadie and Pembroke Jones, seasonal residents of "The Lodge." The turn-of-the-century owners of the sprawling subdivision now known as Landfall were known for hosting lavish and imaginative parties at their Italianate villa designed by John Russell Pope, Pembroke Jones's son-in-law and the architect of the Jefferson Memorial in Washington, D.C.

The hunting lodge, or "Bungalow," as Pembroke Jones called it, was located near the Temple of Love, a coquina gazebo once encircled by four pools.

Like sleight-of-hand on a giant scale, some buildings have left one location only to appear in another. On the corner is the 1740 Smith-Anderson house, Wilmington's oldest dwelling. Dr. Anderson's tiny office was moved about 1889 to the rear of the corner house to make way for the structure seen on the left. Later, the house with the gazebo was demolished, and Dr. Anderson's office was returned to its original site.

The William Belvedere Meares House at 152 North Front Street was built mid-nineteenth century on the site currently occupied by the post office and moved to 418 South Front Street in 1889. According to local architectural historian Edward Turberg, it probably was rolled on logs to flatbed streetcars, which then carried it six blocks to its new location.

Sometimes just part of a building moves to a new location. The large building in the center of this 1914 photograph is the 1843 Custom House designed by John S. Norris. The mantels later were installed in the Martin-Crouch House at 520 Dock Street.

"Light and airy living room; disappearing staircase . . .," the real estate ad might have read in 1973 for this dilapidated building on South Water Street. Mr. and Mrs. Thomas H. Wright Jr., local pioneers of historic preservation and adaptive use, had the structure moved to Chandler's Wharf in the 1980s. The top blew off en route, but the remodeled first floor now houses Scott Rhodes Jewelers.

Honorees at the 1954 dedication of Hugh MacRae Park were, from left to right, county commissioner Claude O'Shields, Agnes MacRae Morton, Rena N. MacRae, and commissioner Ralph Horton. The 101-acre park was a 1924 gift to New Hanover County from Mr. MacRae, who wished for it to remain an unadorned pine forest.

During the directorship of Janet Seapker, shown here in September 1980, armed with one of 30,000 artifacts, Cape Fear Museum has sharpened its focus from the world to a 50-mile radius of Wilmington. In 1992, New Hanover County dedicated its new and improved 42,000-square-foot museum.

The Rt. Reverend Thomas H. Wright and Wilmington businessman Bruce Barclay Cameron were caught in a rare moment at Grandfather Mountain Lake, about 1987. Bishop Wright shepherded the Episcopal Diocese of East Carolina from 1945 until 1972. Jaunty Bruce Cameron and his family are well known for their enterprise and philanthropy.

C.D. Spangler and North Carolina Supreme Court Justice Chief James Exum presided at the installation of Chancellor James Leutze in 1991. What began in 1947 as Wilmington College, a two-year college in Isaac Bear School, is now the University of North Carolina at Wilmington, located on 650 acres of land and housed in 81 buildings. The original architectural design for the campus was the work of Wilmington architect Leslie N. Boney.

This photo was taken from Claude Howell's balcony, looking northwest from Fifth and Market, *c.* 1921. The two gracious homes in the foreground, the McClammy and Beery houses, have now made way for the New Hanover County Law Enforcement Center. Other changes are good examples of a line from a 1970s Joni Mitchell song, " . . . paved paradise, put up a parking lot."

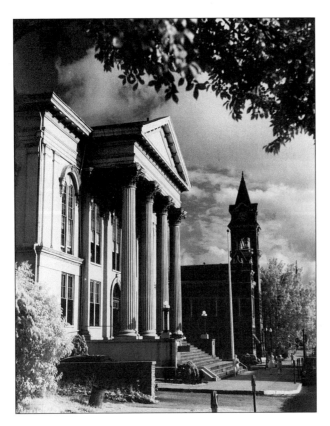

Despite wrecking balls and tongues of flames, much remains that is "picture perfect," like this scenic stretch of North Third Street.

Select Bibliography

Block, Susan. *The Wrights of Wilmington*. Wilmington, 1992.

Campbell, Walter E. *Across Fortune's Tracks: A Biography of William Rand Kenan, Jr.* Chapel Hill University of North Carolina Press, 1996.

Cashman, Diane Cobb. *Cape Fear Adventure: An Illustrated History of Wilmington*. Woodland Hills, California, 1982.

———. *Headstrong: The Biography of Amy Morris Bradley (1823–1904)*. Wilmington, 1990.

Cashman, Diane Cobb and Jean Poole. *The Lonely Road*. Wilmington, 1976.

Davis, Patsy, chairperson. *Wilmington Fire Department, 1897–1955*. Dallas, 1985.

Dunn, G.N. "Wilmington Shipyard Sites, 1860–1970." Special Collections, New Hanover County Public Library.

Fales, Robert M. *Wilmington Yesteryear*. 1984.

Fonvielle, Dr. Chris E. *The Wilmington Campaign*. Campbell, California, 1997.

Hall, Lewis Philip. *Land of the Golden River (I)*. Wilmington, 1975.

Herring, Ethel and Carolee Williams. *Fort Caswell in War and Peace*. Wendell, North Carolina, 1983.

Hewlett, Crockette W. *Two Centuries of Art in New Hanover County*. Durham, 1976.

Hicks, Eugene C. *Hicks, Ward, Wright, le Yonge, and 7,812 Descendants*. Wilmington, 1982.

Hill City Directories. Special Collections, New Hanover County Public Library.

Hudson, Arthur Palmer. *Songs of the Carolina Charter Colonists*. Raleigh, 1962.

Lee, Lawrence. *The History of Brunswick County, North Carolina*. Charlotte, 1980.

———. *The Lower Cape Fear in Colonial Days*. Chapel Hill, 1965.

———. "The Military Career of James Reilly." (Unpublished manuscript.)

Lefler, Hugh and Albert Newsome. *The History of a Southern State*. Chapel Hill, 1973.

McKoy, Henry Bacon. *Wilmington, North Carolina—Do You Remember When?* Greenville, South Carolina, 1957.

Moore, Louis T. *Stories Old and New of the Cape Fear Region*. Wilmington, 1968.

New Hanover County Planning Department. *Historic Architecture of New Hanover County, North Carolina*. Wilmington, 1986.

Powell, William S. *North Carolina through Four Centuries*. Chapel Hill, 1989.

Russell, Anne. *Portraits of Faith*. Norfolk, 1981.

———. *Wilmington, a Pictorial History*. Norfolk, 1981.

Saunders, William L., ed. *Colonial Records of North Carolina*. Raleigh, 1888.

Seapker, Janet and Edward F. Turberg. "Historic Architecture of the Cape Fear." Wilmington, 1985.

Shaffer, E.T.H. *Carolina Gardens*. New York, 1963.

Sprunt, James. *Chronicles of the Lower Cape Fear*. Wilmington, 1992.

Sprunt, James Laurence. *The Story of Orton Plantation*. Wilmington, 1958.

Stamp Defiance Chapter, NSDAR. *Wilmington, Historic Colonial City*. Wilmington, 1952. (Lower Cape Fear Historical Society Archives.)

Star News Files. (Microfilm copies) Special Collections, New Hanover County Public Library.

Stick, David. *Bald Head*. Wendell, North Carolina, 1985.

Turnquist, Robert. *The Packard Story*. New York, 1965.

U.S. Navy Department. *Civil War Naval Chronology, IV*. Washington, D.C., 1966.

Watson, Alan D. *Society in Colonial North Carolina*. Raleigh, 1996.

William L. deRosset. *Wilmington: The Port City of North Carolina*. Wilmington, 1937. (Lower Cape Fear Historical Society Archives.)

Wrenn, Tony P. *Wilmington, North Carolina: An Architectural and Historical Portrait*. Charlottesville: UP of Virginia, 1984.

Photograph Donors

Wilmington Star News; *Wilmington Journal*; North Carolina Division Archives and History; North Carolina State Museum of Natural History Collection; University of North Carolina, North Carolina Collection; Duke University, Perkins Library Special Collections; Amon Carter Museum, Fort Worth, Texas; New Hanover County Library, Special Collections; Mrs. Joseph H. Price; A.J. Howell; Frances Hearn Grover; Henry J. MacMillan; Barbara Marcroft; Margaret Moore Perdew; Henrietta H. Adams; Laura Howell Norden Schorr; Katherine B. Von Glahn; William C. Von Glahn; Henry B. Rehder; Milo A. Manly; Bertha B. Todd; Thomas Hoke Hall; George Nevens; Nathaniel Bost; Elizabeth W. Aiken; Jane MacMillan Rhett; Louise deRosset Smith; Elinor R. Haines; Thomas A. Price; Skinny and Anna Pennington; Katherine R. Symmes; Deanes and Mary Murchison Gornto; Curtis Matthews; Emma Woodward MacMillan; Lucile S. Goldberg; Betty Foy Taylor; Charles H. Foard; Alice Lee Bulluck; Beadie E. Britt; Henry Bacon McKoy; J.E.L. Wade; Joseph W. and Betty Hill Taylor; Robert Chesnutt II; Larry B. Lee; Arthur Bluethenthal; First Citizens Bank (William Golder); Regina King; Jack Dermid; Hugh Morton; Helen Messick Willetts; Bill Reaves; Margaret Hall; C.H. MacDonald; H.O. MacDonald; E.A. Swain; Miss Hayden; Ethel V. Botesky; Martha Bellamy King; Mary Frances Divine; Marilyn Devany Pierce; George Clark; Louise Elliott; W.H. McEachern III; Ida B. Kellam; Mary Amelia Willson; Sadie S. Block; Lucretia T. McDaniel; Margaret M. Baham; Preston Artis; Grace Russ; Dorothy Richards Terrell; Louise deRosset Smith; Augusta M. Cooper; Kathryn J. Jackson; Rose Picot; Aaron May; Frederick L. Block; Wilmington Fire Department; Lizzie Crider; Sandy Mitchell; Miles Higgins; Catherine A. Solomon; Everett Huggins; Claude Howell; Jean Graham; University of North Carolina at Wilmington; James B. Swails; Aileen Hill; Stanley Rehder; Lillian Sebrell Paso; Elaine Warshauer; Lula Foyster; Willa D. Hatcher; and Mary Ann Hogue.